Fascinating FaCts

The EARTH

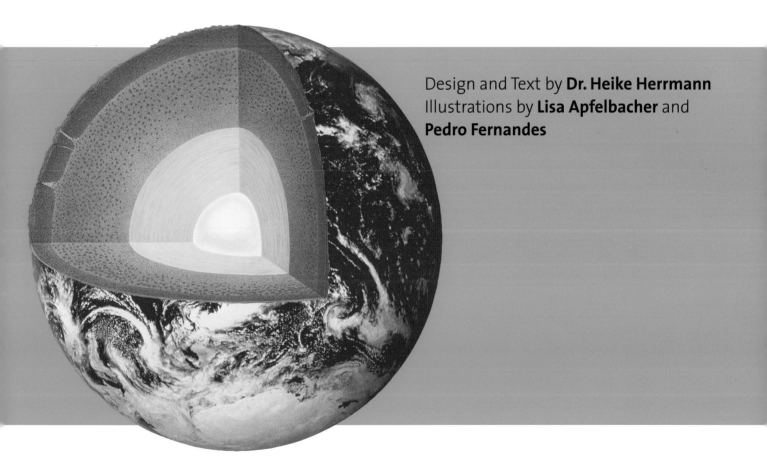

Design and Text by **Dr. Heike Herrmann**
Illustrations by **Lisa Apfelbacher** and
Pedro Fernandes

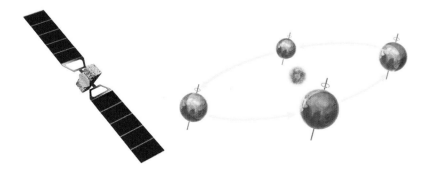

Contents

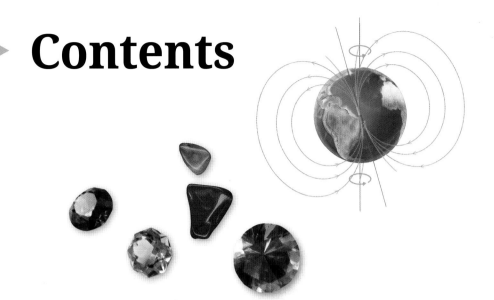

The Earth from afar

Mankind's home planet is a marvellous habitat in the middle of the universe and is fascinating when viewed from space.

6

Extreme forces of nature

Be it a tornado, a hurricane or an earthquake, there is not much that human beings can do in the face of these forces of nature. A good warning system is a help.

34

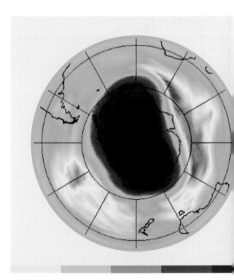

▶ The Earth up close 4

▶ The Earth from afar 6

▶ Sun, Moon and Earth 8

▶ Explorers and astronomers 10

▶ The Earth in the universe 12

▶ The continents 14

▶ Mountains and rocks 16

▶ Erosion and cave formation 18

▶ Reading maps 20

▶ Atmosphere, wind and weather 22

▶ Water circulation 24

▶ Climate and climate zones 26

Fascinating

Author: **Dr. Heike Herrmann**
is a biologist and writes non-fiction books for children and teen-agers. She has also worked as a natural science lecturer for many years.

Specialist consultant: **Prof. Dr. Werner Buggisch**
was Professor of Geology at the University of Erlangen-Nuremberg. His interest in making the natural sciences accessible for children has led to him writing or being involved in the writing of several books for children and teenagers.

Illustrators:
Lisa Apfelbacher studied Forestry and Environmental Science at the University of Freiburg and currently works as an illustrator.
Pedro Fernandes has been working as an illustrator and freelance artist since 2000.

Reading maps

A holiday trip, a city tour, a GPS device is almost always to hand. We ought to still be able to read maps today, however.

20

Climate change and protection

Human beings today have an influence on the atmosphere and the climate. The Earth's climate has undergone continual change for millions of years but the changes now appear to be threatening.

40

Nature's records

Swelteringly heat in the deserts and freezing cold in the polar regions, seemingly unending rivers and enormous caves – the Earth provides astonishing extremes.

46

▶ Polar regions, tundra, forest and steppe 28

▶ Deserts, coastlines, oceans and lakes 30

▶ Volcanoes – the Earth breathing fire .. 32

▶ Extreme forces of nature 34

▶ The origin of life on Earth 36

▶ The Earth as man's habitat 38

▶ Climate change and protection 40

▶ Natural resources and renewable energy 42

▶ Farmland and water 44

▶ Nature's records 46

▶ Index of key words 48

The Earth up close

We get up in the morning and have breakfast, take the bus to school perhaps. That is the normal every-day routine. If we were to think about our world more carefully, however, we would not even get as far as getting up: we would have to ask ourselves why we were able to lie in bed so comfortably instead of floating in the room like astronauts. In fact, where does the oxygen we breathe come from? Or we would have to think about why the Sun always shines into our room from the east in the morning. And so it would go on the whole day. Now it is time to answer many of these questions!

The habitat on Earth
Only air, water and earth are able to support and sustain life, at least life as we know it.

Is the Earth the only planet supporting life?

The Earth is indeed the only planet known to us on which life is possible. Space probes have been sent to the neigh-bouring planets of Venus and Mars but nowhere within our solar system have we been able to find a definite sign of life, neither in the past nor at present. We do know for certain that other solar systems have planets, however, and this raises the question of whether there might not be life there – perhaps even intelligent life. It is indeed possible that, on another planet somewhere in the expanse of the universe, someone else is sitting there with some kind of telescope, discovering the Earth and asking themselves exactly the same question!

The image of the Earth up close is characterised by a great many colours.

An "artificial" biosphere

In 1991 scientists attempted to build an artificial atmosphere. They wanted to create a self-sustaining system independent of the world outside and one in which life is possible on a long term basis. The smallest members of the project, the microorganisms, were responsible for the project's failure, however. They reproduced so rapidly that they deprived the other living organisms of oxygen.

Where on our planet is life able to exist?

The flat Earth
In Antiquity many people believed that the Earth was flat.

Living organisms exist on Earth in a wide variety of environments. Bacteria are also found in hot springs, and there are algae even under the polar ice. Signs of life have even been found at the deepest point in the ocean, the Mariana Trench located at a depth of about 11,000 m, and the maximum flight altitude of birds is around 8000 m. Nevertheless, the area in which the majority of life forms are found is not very large. It extends from the upper soil layer up to a height of around 5000 m. In their entirety, all of the zones in which life is able to exist are called the biosphere. This is also where all of the chemical substances essential for life are to be found.

What does the Earth look like on the inside?

The solid earth on which we stand forms part of the Earth's continental crust. The oceanic crust lies beneath the world's oceans. Beneath that is the Earth's mantle, the upper layer of which is viscous. The lower layer of the Earth's mantle is solid owing to the pressure of the rock lying on top of it. There are "convection currents" within the Earth's mantle as a result of the rock becoming heated at great depths, then rising and cooling and then sinking again. This causes the movement of the continental plates on the Earth's crust. The liquid outer layer of the Earth's core is beneath the Earth's mantle. It comprises molten iron and nickel. The Earth's core is made of solid metal.

We stand on the Earth's solid crust, while much of what is beneath the crust is in molten liquid form.

The Earth is not exactly spherical. The Equator, a circle that is equidistant from both poles (40,000 km in length, 12,756 km in diameter), divides the Earth into two hemispheres. The Earth is comprised of several layers, like an onion, the matter with the greatest density being at the Earth's core and lighter rock layers closer to the Earth's surface:

(1) **Earth's crust:**
Continental crust, around 30–60 km thick, up to 700 °C;
Oceanic crust, around 5–10 km thick, up to 700 °C

Earth's mantle:
(2) Upper mantle, about 600 km thick, up to 1300 °C;
(3) Lower mantle, about 2200 km thick, up to 2800 °C

Earth's core:
(4) Outer core, about 2300 km thick, up to 3700 °C;
(5) Inner core, about 1200 km thick, up to 4000–5000 °C

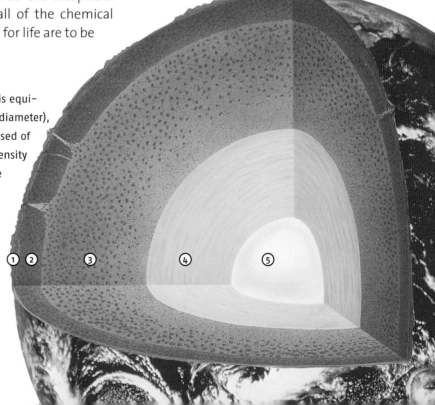

The Earth from afar

Many things are a matter of perspective: if you are standing in the midst of events you see exactly what is going on directly around you. If you step back a little, you then have a good overview of your surroundings. This is exactly the same for astronauts and scientists observing the Earth from space, whether from a spaceship or with the help of satellite images. For example, they are able to observe the links between weather conditions, determine climate developments and changes in nature that perhaps affect the entire planet.

What can you see of the Earth from space?

Satellites "observe" the Earth 24 hours a day. They have many purposes. Weather satellites record weather conditions. Navigation satellites are used for determining positions on Earth. Earth observation satellites photograph the Earth and the images help cartographers to produce maps. Scientists are able to observe environmental changes. The military uses spy satellites in order to monitor troop movements. And anyone can view the place where they live from above on the internet.

Satellite images of the Eyjafjallajökull volcano

The columns of ash from the Eyjafjallajökull volcano in Iceland sometimes reached heights of up to eleven kilometres and even paralysed air traffic in Europe.

What does the Earth look like to an astronaut?

A bright blue planet with layers of white, majestic, beautiful and fragile in the blackness of space – astronauts wax lyri-

The Earth as seen from space: a fascinating blue-white planet

A view of the Earth at night: the dots of light indicate heavily built-up areas.

cal when they describe the Earth. They all agree that they return to Earth in awe. It is only from space that we realise that the seemingly big Earth is in fact small and delicate. On the Earth itself we only have an overview of our immediate surroundings, perhaps of the clearing of a lovely area of forest. The devastating extent of environmental destruction becomes evident from above, however; it becomes clear just how much of the threatened rainforests have in fact already been destroyed.

Astronauts at work on the International Space Station, ISS. The Earth is always in view from there.

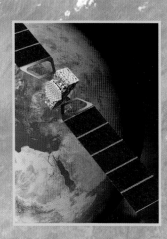

A navigation satellite enables the precise determining of position to within a matter of centimetres.

A meteorite landed on the Earth here about 15 million years ago.

Do flying objects from space reach us?

In all probability we have not yet been visited by aliens from space. Alien rock fragments repeatedly approach the Earth, however. Small fragments burn up in the atmosphere as shooting stars (meteors). Larger fragments do not burn up completely and pieces of them reach the Earth. These pieces are known as meteorites. A huge meteorite landed on the Earth some 65 million years ago. A huge cloud of ash and dust swirled up into the atmosphere, darkening the sky. A great many animals and plants died out, including the dinosaurs.

Why is the Earth called the Blue Planet?

It is only from a distance that the Earth appears as the Blue Planet. The Earth's surface is covered by three large oceans, the Atlantic Ocean, the Pacific Ocean and the Indian Ocean. Two thirds of the Earth's surface is covered with water. The oceans are an important driving force for the climate and the temperature differences between day and night would be much greater without the oceans' ability to store heat. The evaporation from the oceans also provides the precipitation without which life on Earth would be impossible.

The first human being in space
The Russian cosmonaut Yuri Gagarin was the first human being in space.

7

Sun, Moon and Earth

The interaction between these three celestial bodies influences life on Earth in a multitude of ways. The movements of the Earth, the Moon and the Sun form the basis for our measurement of time. The Earth orbits the Sun within the space of a year. A lunar month is the period of time between one full moon phase and the next. And the Earth takes about 24 hours to revolve once around its own axis. The tides, too, high tide and low tide, are caused by the position of the celestial bodies in relation to one another.

What causes the seasons?

We are all familiar with spring, summer, autumn and winter – but why do they occur? They are caused by the tilting of the Earth's axis towards the orbit of the Sun. This means that the Sun does not shine on the Earth with equal strength all year round. When orbiting the Sun, the respective hemispheres of the Earth sometimes lean towards the Sun and sometimes lean away from it. If the northern hemisphere is tilted towards the Sun then the Sun's rays reach the Earth at a steeper angle and a great deal of solar energy reaches that hemisphere. It is summer. The Sun is high up in the sky at midday. It is warm and the days are long. It is now winter in the southern hemisphere. If the northern hemisphere is tilted away from the Sun then the Sun's rays fall at a shallow angle. Now it is winter here. The Sun is still low in the sky even at midday, it is noticeably cooler, and the days are short. Further north the Sun does not even rise at all. It is then dark at the north pole for half of the year. The two hemispheres receive roughly the same amount of summer in the spring and autumn.

A tree changing with the seasons

This is a familiar sight for many people: nature changing with the seasons.

Seasons

The northern and southern hemispheres are separated by the Equator. It "divides" the Earth into two hemispheres. Both the northern and the southern hemispheres lean more towards the Sun once during the course of a single year. The sequence of the seasons in the northern hemisphere is as follows (the sequence is in the reverse order in the southern hemisphere):

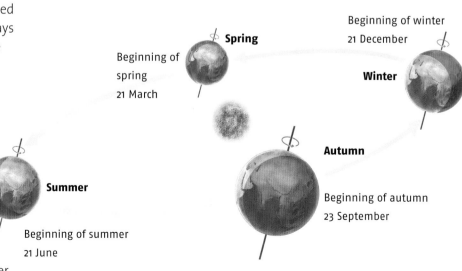

Beginning of spring 21 March — **Spring**

Beginning of winter 21 December — **Winter**

Beginning of autumn 23 September — **Autumn**

Beginning of summer 21 June — **Summer**

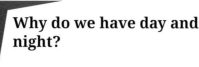

Why do we have day and night?

The Sun "rises" in the east and "sets" in the west. This is a saying learnt by many children. But does the Sun really rise and set? The Earth revolves once around itself from west to east in about 24 hours. In the morning we revolve towards the Sun and in the evening we revolve away from it. It therefore only looks as if the Sun rises and sets. You can try this out easily using a lamp as the Sun and a small ball as the Earth.

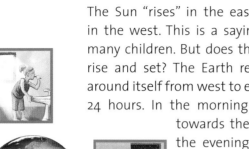

Day and night
The whole of our daily routine is determined by the alternation between day and night.

High and low tide
High tide occurs when the sea level is high, while low tide is when the water recedes and the sea level drops. Large differences between high and low tide can even cause ships to be grounded.

What causes the tides?

Anyone who has ever been to the sea knows about high and low tide. But what is it that moves the water? All solid objects exert a certain gravitational force. This also applies to the Moon and the Sun and they therefore cause the masses of water making up the oceans to move as well. The water on the side of the Earth facing the Moon is subjected to an especially strong pull by the Moon and forms a high tide. On the other side of the Earth a second high tide is caused by centrifugal force. Centrifugal force is caused by the rotation of the Earth and the Moon around a common centre of gravity. The Earth revolves around its own axis faster than the Moon orbits around the Earth and so the Earth revolves through the tides.

The Earth as a magnet
The Earth is surrounded by a magnetic field that acts as a protective shield. It deflects dangerous, high-energy particles from the Sun.

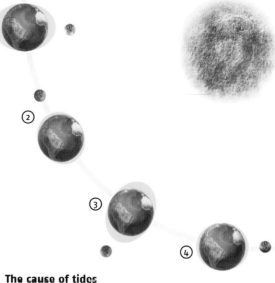

The cause of tides
① The Moon and the Sun are in line with one another and their gravitational forces combine. This produces high tides that become spring tides.
② and ④ The Moon and the Sun are at right angles to the Earth, partially cancelling out their gravitational force. The high tides are lower and become neap tides.
③ The Moon and the Sun are in line with one another and their gravitational forces are reinforced. This causes high tides that become spring tides.

Is the Earth a magnet?

Everyone knows that the early seafarers were very good at orientating themselves using a compass. This means, however, that the Earth must behave like a magnet and this is indeed the case. The currents in the metallic, liquid outer part of the Earth's core are probably the source of the Earth's magnetic fields. Like a bar magnet, the Earth, too, has two magnetic poles. They do not correspond exactly to the geographic poles, however.

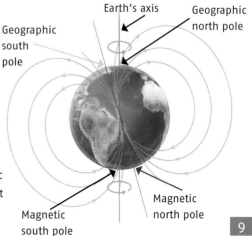

Earth's axis

Geographic north pole

Geographic south pole

Magnetic north pole

Magnetic south pole

Explorers and astronomers

Explorers and astronomers have continually found and described new things during the course of history. Discovering unknown areas of the Earth had started to become difficult by the start of the last century because most of the Earth had already been explored. It is no longer possible today that unknown islands will suddenly appear on the horizon after many days at sea. It is only the deep sea that still offers really "new territory". Astronomists, who cast their eyes into the depths of the universe, have it easier because there is clearly still an infinite amount to discover there.

Antarctic research today and around 100 years ago – left the German Neumayer Station III, right **Robert Falcon Scott** with his companions at the south pole.

The British seafarer **James Cook** discovered many South Sea Islands.

Have there always been explorers?

Today we have off-road vehicles, aircraft and many kinds of ships. It is therefore sometimes hard to imagine how people set off on discovery expeditions several thousand years ago. We do know, however, that even in the very distant past people continually set out to discover new territories. The Vikings from the north reached the American mainland with astoundingly simple boats in around the year 1000.

Replica of a Viking ship

What was the reason for discovery expeditions?

Curiosity and inquiring minds were certainly one important reason. Often, however, it was also about finding new trade routes. A great many such journeys were also commissioned by rulers aspiring to gain more power and especially greater wealth. They provided the money for the expeditions.

What happened to the new territories and the people?

Most of the inhabitants of the discovered territories would have preferred to have remained undiscovered. The majority were suppressed with unimaginable cruelty and exploited. Some of those expelled from their territory still suffer from the consequences today, for example the Indians of North America.

The versatile natural scientist **Alexander von Humboldt** brought together knowledge from many areas of the Earth.

Galileo Galilei built his tele-scope to observe the skies.

This early astronomi-cal instrument is known as a planetary machine or "orrery". The astronomist **Tycho Brahe** worked with one of these in the 16th century.

The latest technology at the time, now in a museum: telescopes were used as of the 17th century. They have been developed further over the course of time.

Telescope on the Canary Island of La Palma
The silver sphere contains an ultramodern telescope. Its reflector has a diameter of 10.4 m, making it one of the largest ever.

Why is astronomy so commonplace?

Astronomy is concerned with the "laws of the stars". Anyone who regularly looks up at the night sky asks themselves questions about space and time, the Earth and space. We know that a kind of calendar was used as far back as the late Stone Age. Be it Egypt, Greece or China, astronomy has played an important role in all major civilisations, forming part of science and religion.

How does astronomy change our view of the world?

Astronomical observations do not allow us to see everything from the outside because we ourselves are right in the midst. This means that misjudgements are easily made. The "geocentric world view" goes back to the astronomers of Ancient Greece who saw the Earth as the focal point orbited by the Sun and the planets. It was only in around 1500 that Johannes Kepler and Nicolaus Copernicus were able to enforce the "heliocentric world view" with the Sun at the centre. It was then Albert Einstein and his Theory of Relativity who introduced a new concept of space and time in the 20th century.

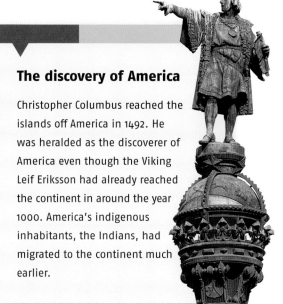

The discovery of America

Christopher Columbus reached the islands off America in 1492. He was heralded as the discoverer of America even though the Viking Leif Eriksson had already reached the continent in around the year 1000. America's indigenous inhabitants, the Indians, had migrated to the continent much earlier.

What technology do astronomers use?

Astronomy had already seen a great many interesting instruments by the time the first telescope was built in 1608, this being a further milestone. It was devel-oped further by the Italian natural sci-entist and astronomist Galileo Galilei as well as by Johannes Kepler for their own purposes. The astronomical telescope has since been subject to continual improve-ment. An entirely different technology was developed in the last century based on the fact that the Sun and other objects emit radio waves. Radio telescopes are able to receive and then evaluate these waves.

The Earth in the universe

If there was a spaceship that could fly people to the edge of our galaxy then the space travellers would be able to see with their own eyes everything that we instead have to piece together with a great deal of effort from many individual observations: the structure of our galaxy and the position of our planetary system in the Milky Way, the position of the Earth in the planetary system and a great deal more. For example, scientists have to use enormous reflectors or radio telescopes to try and find out more about our Earth's surroundings.

Where is our solar system located within the universe?

We have to think in terms of huge dimensions when it comes to the universe. Our solar system is a tiny part of a galaxy known as the Milky Way. Our Sun, without which we would be unable to survive, is just one of about 200 billion stars in this galaxy. The light from the Sun takes about 8 minutes to reach the Earth and about 100,000 years to cross the whole of the Milky Way. What that really means becomes clear when you think about the fact that light travels at 300,000 km per second.

The Milky Way, our home galaxy: the solar system of which the Earth forms part is located in a spiral arm away from the centre of the Milky Way.

Looking at the Moon with binoculars

You can discover interesting details on the Moon just by using binoculars. When the moon is waxing or waning you can clearly see high mountains along the shadowy edge and the large craters. You can also see the distinct outlines of the "moon seas".

Why is the Milky Way a strip in the sky?

As early as 1609 the famous physicist Galileo Galilei recognised that the bright clouds making up the Milky Way are a collection of stars. Only later did it become clear why the Milky Way appears to us as a strip in the sky. It is shaped like a disc. If we were able to sit on the disc ourselves and look along the disc we would see the many stars as a bright strip.

The Earth as the Blue Planet
From a distance we can clearly see that 70 % of the Earth is covered with water. The atmosphere encloses the Earth as shimmering blue layer.

Our planetary system

① Neptune ② Uranus ③ Saturn ④ Jupiter ⑤ Mars ⑥ Earth ⑦ Venus ⑧ Mercury

According to the latest information Pluto is not a planet and is instead one of the dwarf planets.

View of the Earth from the Moon

The Earth rises above the horizon of the Moon.

Where is the Earth within our planetary system?

The Earth is about 150 million kilometres from the Sun. The Sun's rays carry enough energy to make life on Earth possible but without being so strong that all the water would evaporate. The Earth's mass is also important because it means that the Earth's gravitational force is strong enough to hold down the atmosphere essential to life.

Why is the Moon so important for the Earth?

Things were fairly rough during the time that the planetary system came into being. The tilt of the Earth's axis is the result of a large celestial body impacting on the Earth. The collision sent large quantities of matter spinning off into space, matter that then compacted over time to form our Moon. If the Moon did not stabilise the Earth's rotational axis with its gravitational force, the Earth would "wobble" terribly and there would be tremendous climate fluctuations.

What is gravity?

Gravity is the property by which physical bodies are able to attract one another. It is dependant on the mass of the physical bodies and on their distance from one another. The Earth's gravitational pull keeps the Moon in its orbit. If the Earth's gravitational pull were to suddenly disappear the Moon would fly away from the Earth.

Earth's gravitational pull

As a heavy body, the Earth attracts every other physical body. As the Earth is almost spherical in shape, the force is concentrated at the centre of the Earth.

The continents

The Earth provides a reliable picture when you look at a globe: here is Australia, there is America, and there is Italy with its boot-shaped outline. While we are looking at this image of our Earth, however, all of this is moving, infinitely slowly in our terms yet driven by a tremendous energy. The plates of the Earth's solid outer shell move about 2 to 20 cm per year. The catastrophic earthquake in Japan in 2011 was also the result of these shifts.

According to present day theories, our Earth began with the "Big Bang".

How long has the Earth been there?

When scientists write about the history and the development of the Earth they usually talk in terms of millions and billions of years. This indicates the dimensions involved. Scientists today are of the opinion that our Earth and the other planets were formed about 4600 million years ago from a giant cloud of dust and debris that became more and more compacted. Size, distance from the Sun, the nature of the matter – it is astounding how many conditions had to match perfectly in order for our planet to become what it is.

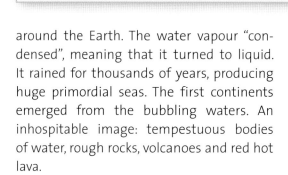

The San Andreas Fault

The San Andreas Fault in America is about 1100 km long and extends from Mexico to the north of San Francisco. Here the Pacific Plate and the North American Plate slide past one another at a speed of about 6 cm per year.

around the Earth. The water vapour "condensed", meaning that it turned to liquid. It rained for thousands of years, producing huge primordial seas. The first continents emerged from the bubbling waters. An inhospitable image: tempestuous bodies of water, rough rocks, volcanoes and red hot lava.

What did the Earth look like in the past?

Over time, the Earth's core was formed from the heavy elements iron and nickel, with a mantle of lighter elements around it and finally a thin crust. The gases pouring out of the volcanoes produced a gas shell devoid of oxygen

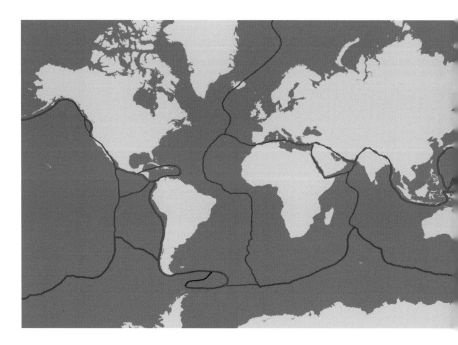

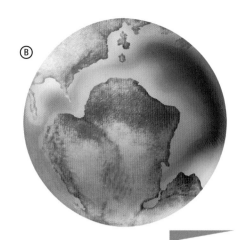
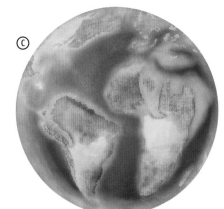
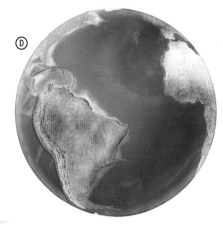

The breaking up of a super-continent

(A) About 200 million years ago all of the land masses were combined as a single continent named Pangaea.

(B) This supercontinent broke in two about 150 million years ago: Laurasia (upper section in the picture) and Gondwana.

(C) About 100 million years ago Laurasia broke up into North America and Eurasia, Gondwana into South America, Africa, the Antarctic, Australia and India.

(D) The continents as we know them today.

What are the tectonic plates?

The Earth's solid, outer crust is not completely sealed but is divided up into sections. You can think of it like the shell of a boiled egg that has been smashed. The pieces are referred to as tectonic plates. Today there are seven large sections: the Pacific and the Antarctic Plates, the North and the South American Plates as well as the African, Eurasian and the Australian Plates. There are also more than 20 small plates and a great many micro-plates. These support the ocean floors (oceanic crust) as well as the continents (oceanic and continental crusts).

Where do the plates move to?

All of the plates, i.e. the whole "shell", float on the viscous rock making up the Earth's upper mantle. They are moved by the currents and the turbulence in the Earth's mantle. The heat from the centre of the Earth keeps this constant movement going. Scientists are now able to predict plate movements. It would appear that in many millions of years from now, we will be able to drive from Europe to Australia by car. The only question is whether there will still be any cars then.

Tectonic plates

The black lines indicate the outlines of the tectonic plates. The subduction zones run along the red lines.

—— Tectonic plates

—— Subduction zones

The theory of continental drift

The theory is that of the German geologist, meteorologist and polar explorer Alfred Wegener (1880–1930). He determined that today's continents derived from a large continent because they fit together like pieces of a puzzle.

① **East African Rift Valley** Two continental plates are drifting apart. Faults develop, volcanoes erupt and earthquakes occur.

② **Mid-Atlantic Ridge** When two oceanic plates drift apart the Earth's crust is torn open and hot molten rock rises to the surface forming a new ocean floor.

③ **The Andes** When an oceanic plate collides with a continental plate the heavier oceanic plate sinks beneath the continental plate into the Earth's mantle. This is known as subduction. Mountains are formed, such as the Andes for example, volcanoes develop and there are frequent earthquakes.

④ **The Alps** When two equally heavy plates collide then the one plate does not simply slide beneath the other, instead the plates push against each other and fold upwards. This produces a mountain range such as the Alps.

⑤ **The San Andreas Fault** Two plates rubbing against one another can become caught. Earthquakes occur when they then slide free again.

Mountains and rocks

Stones are a common feature of our surroundings and mankind has probably been using them for as long as there have been human beings on Earth. Flint, for example, was a sought-after object for barter for thousands of years. It was used to make spear and arrowheads. Humans build stone houses, use clay, sand, marble and gravel. Mountain chains like the Alps, the Rocky Mountains or the Himalayas tower up out of masses of rock. Yet even though rock seems to us to be very hard and stable, it is constantly changing. Weathering by wind, water, ice, plants and microorganisms shapes rocks and creates fissures in mountains.

How are mountains formed?

It is easy to imagine how mountains are formed if you think about tectonic plate movement. If two equally heavy plates collide then the rocks at this point are pushed up on top of one another, folded and raised. You can try this out with a simple experiment. If you slowly push the two ends of a towel spread out on a smooth surface towards the middle, folds are formed. The Alps, for example, fold upwards because this is where the African plate collides with the Eurasian Plate. There are also zones in which a heavier oceanic plate slides under a lighter continental plate, also causing mountains to tower up. This process is accompanied by significant volcanic activity as well as earthquakes.

Many climbers pursue their hobby in the Alps.

The Andes are a good example of this kind of mountain formation. Here, the Pacific Plate sinks beneath the South American Plate.

Why do mountains not grow right up into the heavens?

The plates are constantly moving and so you would think that the upward folding of a mountain chain would simply go on and on with the mountains rising higher and higher. The first part is true: the plates are continually busy folding. Weathering, however, prevents mountains from becoming higher and higher.

Tremendous sideways pressure can even cause layers of rock to fold.

Precious stones

Precious stones are minerals and are formed under very particular conditions within rocks. They often occur as crystals. Well known precious stones are rubies, sapphires, emeralds and diamonds. The minerals only become gemstones once they have been specially cut and polished.

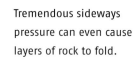
①

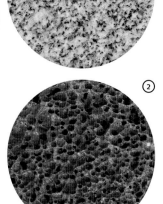
②

The Alps began to form more than 80 million years ago. The Alps are in fact still very young for mountains.

Different rocks

Igneous rocks:
① Granite ② Basalt
Sedimentary rocks:
③ Sandstone
Metamorphic rocks:
④ Marble ⑤ Slate

③

④

⑤

What does weathering mean?

Weathering breaks rock into smaller pieces but it also changes it. Differences in temperature between summer and winter or between day and night make rock brittle. Frozen water causes it to expand. The pressure that builds up when ice forms in rock fissures causes whole sections of rock to break off. Water also sets off chemical reactions and is thus able to corrode rock. Acidic excretions from bacteria or from lichen for example dissolve minerals and destroy the rock's structure.

What is rock?

"Oldest rock on Earth discovered!" was announced in 2008. The 4.28 billion year old find from northern Canada is rather exciting for scientists because the rock could be a piece of our planet's very first crust. The rock might also reveal more about the formation of the first continents. But what is "rock" in fact? It is generally a solid, bonded combination of minerals and the remains of organisms.

Are all rocks the same?

There are three main types of rock. Igneous rocks are formed by the cooling of red hot molten magma. Metamorphic rocks are formed when rock is exposed to pressure or to high temperatures. These conditions are prevalent in the depths of the Earth when a plate sinks, for example. The third type is sedimentary rock. Rock that is worn away is deposited as sediment, such as sand for example, in another place. Over the course of millions of years it is compressed and becomes hard. It is in this way that sand is turned into sandstone and chalky mud into limestone.

The Chateau du Haut Koenigsbourg in Alsace is built out of sandstone blocks.

Erosion and cave formation

The river has cut a huge canyon in the plateau. The sides drop down steeply. This area looked different a few million years ago. How did this new landscape develop? It was caused not only by weathering but also by erosion – the constant wearing away and carrying off of rock and soil by ice, wind and water. Caves are also formed by the impact of water on layers of rock.

What is erosion?

The erosion process is best understood by looking at a fast-flowing river in the mountains. The water has tremendous strength. Stones are carried along, constantly rubbing against one another and being ground down into gravel, sand and mud. The water also constantly wears away matter from the river banks. Where the river flows very fast it sweeps a great many particles along with it. Where the land becomes flatter the river flows more gently and deposits gravel, sand and stones. Rivers are thus constantly levelling the landscape. Whether this ultimately results in a deep gorge, a canyon or a wide valley depends on the rock and the flow rate, amongst other things. The wind is also a strong erosive force. Grains of sand in the air are able to grind down rocks as if a giant had been using a huge piece of sandpaper.

Glaciers "flow" down mountain slopes. They drag earth and loose stones along with them, cutting into rocks and forming a U-shaped valley.

What does farmland have to do with erosion?

There would be no farmland without weathering and erosion. Fertile loess soil, for example, is made up of soil particles ground down by Ice Age glaciers. They were blown away by the wind and deposited somewhere else. The reverse is also true, with wind, rain and water carrying away the layers of top soil again. This is known as soil erosion.

Dunes protect the land from flood waters. They are planted with vegetation to prevent them being carried off by wind and water.

The Grand Canyon

The Grand Canyon in the USA was formed by the Colorado River over the course of millions of years. It extends down to a depth of 1.8 km. Visitors on the viewing platform should therefore have no fear of heights.

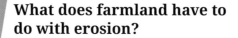

The disappearing Danube

A large quantity of the Danube's waters seep into limestone fissures near Immendingen. The water then flows for about 12 km through a system of underground caves before reaching the Aach spring. From here this water from the Danube flows via Lake Constance into the Rhine, while the rest of the Danube flows into the Black Sea.

How are caves formed?

Most caves are found in limestone mountains and there is a special reason for this. Water alone does not have a particularly strong effect on limestone. Rainwater, however, which has absorbed carbon dioxide from the air or from the soil, contains carbonic acid, which can dissolve limestone. When this water finds its way into cracks and fissures in the rock it consistently dissolves the lime. Over thousands of years this results in wide cracks, underground tunnels and caves that can grow to become gigantic in size. During this process of dissolving the water becomes enriched with a chemical substance known as calcium hydrogen carbonate.

Stalactite or stalagmite?

Caves are a fascinating world beneath the Earth. Water creates the most unusual hollow chambers, it fills streams and crystal clear lakes, and it develops wonderful limestone formations because the process of chemical dissolution also works in the reverse. When water rich in calcium hydrogen carbonate drips down from the roof of a cave, the carbon dioxide escapes and the lime is deposited. A thin layer of lime is formed on the roof, drop by drop, as well as in the place where the drops land. Stalactites thus grow down from the cave roof and stalagmites grow up from the ground. There is an astounding diversity of stalactite and stalagmite forms: fragile translucent curtains, thin spaghetti, large spheres and pearl-shaped deposits.

Limestone cave

What do cave explorers study?

Caves hold a great many surprises as explorers are continually finding traces of past life. Cave drawings tell how Stone Age people hunted animals. Animal bones indicate that cave inhabitants also included cave bears that spent the winter in the protection of caves. Finds comprising human bones, pots and figures show that humans used caves as places of refuge. Scientists have even found a miniature carved mammoth made of mammoth ivory that is about 35,000 years old. A cave explorer needs to be well-equipped: helmet, headlamp, survival blanket, first aid kit, warm clothes and good shoes are essential. Special climbing gear helps in mastering steep sections. You should never explore a cave on your own and without taking someone with experience with you, however.

Craggy caves
Here you clearly need non-tear clothing and climbing gear to explore the cave.

Reading maps

Going on holiday by car these days often means programming the navigation device but up until just a few years ago there were no such easy solutions. You needed to obtain the appropriate maps prior to your journey and were always pleased to have a passenger who was good at "reading" maps. In past centuries there were many areas of the Earth that had not yet been "mapped". They did not appear on any map. In the meantime, however, man has even mapped the Moon!

Who produces maps?

Maps are made by cartographers, or map makers. As you can imagine, here, too, working with a computer plays a very important role. Cartographers are reliant on a great deal of information. They are only able to start work once an area has been properly surveyed. They repeatedly have to incorporate countless changes in order to keep maps right up to date. Now there are of course many maps that no longer get printed but are saved as data.

The prime meridian
The prime meridian passes through Greenwich, an area of London and is the line of longitude defined to be 0°, the starting point for the numbering of the other lines of longitude. Longitude and latitude are the long, classifying lines used for mapping the Earth.

Which map shows what?

Maps can be very different depending on what they are to be used for. The biggest difference is probably that between land and sea maps, with precise information also being required on water. Some land maps give us a good overview of the countries in Europe and indicate the political boundaries. Other maps are made for hiking tours. These are very useful for exploring an area on foot. These maps show viewing points as well as camping and BBQ sites, for example.

Maps
Maps provide an overview of where the larger towns are and where the most important road links run. Anyone taking a close look at a map of England will see the capital London, for instance, the airports nearby and the motorway that circles London.

The **lines of longitude** run from pole to pole. The lines of longitude are counted to the east and to the west around the Earth from the prime meridian.
Latitude: the Equator has the latitude 0° (degrees). The north pole is then 90° north, the south pole 90° south.

Street maps

Street maps are maps used for orientation in an urban area. They are of course characterised by heavily built–up areas and there are less green areas. Cartographers usually try to include the names of even the tiniest of alleyways.

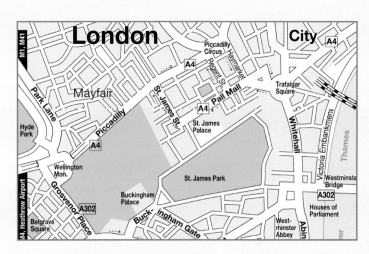

What is a legend?

"Legend" here has nothing to do with stories; it is the key to the symbols on a map. The symbols used are by no means the same on all maps, so you have to know them in order to understand what is shown. How can I tell which are the motorways? How is a rest hut for hikers indicated? What is the symbol indicating a hotel? In order to be able to read a map properly it is also helpful to know that north is generally at the top and also how to convert the scale indicated. A scale of 1:100,000, for example, means that 1 cm on the map is equal to 100,000 cm – i.e. 1 km – in the "real" area.

What is GPS?

GPS is the abbreviation for "global positioning system", a system that was originally set up for the American military. There are more than 20 satellites orbiting the Earth at high altitudes and emitting signals that indicate their precise location in the sky. A GPS (or navigation) device usually receives signals from at least four satellites in order to be able to determine its own position. It is then able to calculate the rest of the route for a car journey, for example. GPS data have now become very important for the production of maps.

The nature of the connection between satellites and a GPS device

Legend (map symbols)

- ═○═ Motorway
- ═══ Dual carriageway
- ┅┅ Railway
- ✈ Airport
- ★ Sightseeing attraction
- ◙ UNESCO World Heritage site

Atmosphere, wind and weather

The Earth's atmosphere is a gas shell. The Earth's gravitational pull keeps the individual gas particles at a specific altitude. The higher up you go, the thinner the air becomes. The particles right at the top escape into space. The interaction between solar energy, air and water vapour in the lowest layer of the atmosphere produces the weather. The atmosphere is essential for our life on Earth. It ensures that it does not get too cold or too hot on Earth, it protects against the Sun's dangerous ultra violet rays and contains the oxygen we breathe.

The weather influences our everyday life, sometimes catching us unawares with a rain shower.

Why is photosynthesis a great invention by nature?

Organisms containing green leaf colour produce sugar and oxygen from carbon dioxide and water with the help of the Sun's energy. This is called photosynthesis. The majority of living creatures need oxygen to breathe. Sugar is the basic nutrient for green organisms themselves but also for all of those that feed on these organisms such as animals and human beings. Solar energy is freely available and carbon dioxide is produced by exhalation, for example.

Composition of air
Air at ground level contains
- 21% oxygen,
- 78% nitrogen,
- 1% trace gases,
- 0.03% carbon dioxide and water vapour.

How was the Earth's atmosphere formed?

About four billion years ago the countless volcanic eruptions led to the formation of a gas shell around the Earth. It was a mixture of water vapour, carbon dioxide, hydrogen sulphide and nitrogen, poisonous for us. The compositions changed repeatedly over the course of the Earth's history. An important change occurred around two billion years ago when the first forms of life producing oxygen developed in the oceans. The oxygen was initially absorbed by the rock but the gas shell became enriched with oxygen over the course of time and our atmosphere as we know it today was formed.

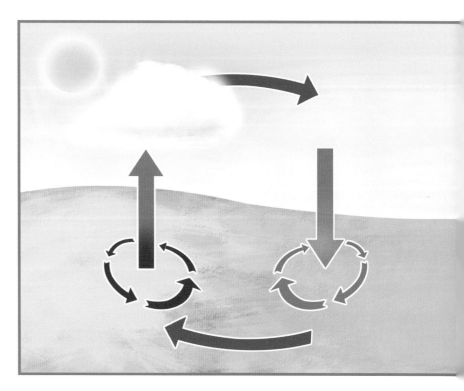

Where is the weather made?

The atmosphere is divided into different layers. The weather occurs in the troposphere. This is where the heating or cooling of the air takes place, air currents are formed, as well as clouds, thunderstorms, rain and hail – namely the weather occurrences as we know them.

From space the atmosphere appears as a thin, bluish shell around the Earth.

How is wind caused?

The Sun is the weather's motor. It heats the ground which then warms the air above it. The air particles then move about more quickly and spread about. The air expands, becomes lighter and rises. Cooler air immediately flows in beneath it. This movement of air is the wind. The air cools down at higher altitudes and clouds form. The air becomes heavier and begins to sink.

Wind circulation
Warm air rises and creates low air pressure (a "low"). Clouds form in the sky when warm air cools. The air becomes heavier. Heavy cold air sinks and creates high air pressure (a "high"). The air flows around the high in the direction of the low.

The atmosphere
The atmosphere is not only essential for humans to breathe it also deflects some of the Sun's heat radiation from the Earth so an average temperature comfortable for living creatures prevails. The ozone layer in the stratosphere also absorbs ("swallows") carcinogenic shortwave UV radiation, thus keeping it away from the Earth.

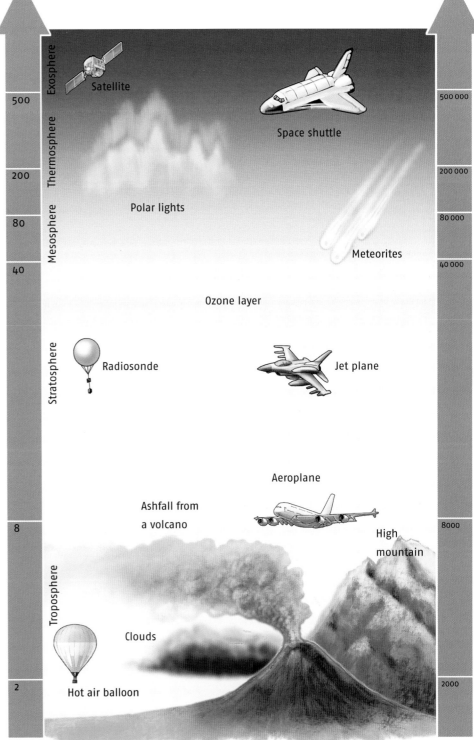

Altitude in kilometres

Altitude in metres

Water circulation

The greatest proportion of water came from the inside of Earth at the time that the Earth was formed. Volcanoes flung water vapour and other gases into the atmosphere, clouds formed, it rained for thousands of years and the oceans were filled. Life as we know it would not be possible without liquid water. Even in Antiquity water was considered one of the four vital elements. It is of particular significance in many religions and a wide variety of scientific disciplines are concerned with water.

Water is constantly circulating between the ocean, the atmosphere and the land.

How does water circulation work?

It rains. Streams, lakes and rivers are filled with water. But where does the rain come from? The Sun's heat warms the air and the ocean waters. The water evaporates and rises together with the warm air. The moist air cools high up in the sky and small droplets of water are formed, producing clouds. The wind blows the clouds towards the land where the water falls back down to Earth as rain, snow or hail. Water on the mainland also evaporates. Some of the rain seeps into the ground, the rest being stored as ice in the polar regions and high mountain ranges. Most of the water flows back into the sea via lakes, streams, rivers and water courses, thus completing the water cycle. The Sun is the force that drives this cycle. Without the Sun the mainland would be dry and there would be no life.

Fresh water reservoir
Polar ice

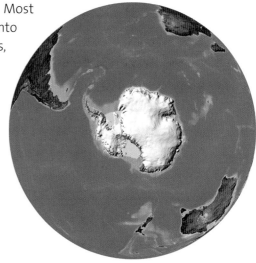

Icebergs from the polar seas regularly drift south, as was the case with the iceberg that collided with the passenger ship the "Titanic".

Basic symbols are used to describe the weather such as sunshine, rain or snow, for example.

What is precipitation?

Precipitation is water in either solid or liquid form that falls to the Earth from the clouds either as hail, sleet, snow or rain. Dew, frost and fog are also considered to be precipitation, however. The form of the precipitation is determined by the atmosphere. In a storm cloud, for instance, strong winds continually carry the water droplets to high altitudes. Ice crystals are formed, around which more and more ice is deposited. At some point they then fall to the Earth as hailstones. For it to snow, it has to be cold not only in the upper layers of the air but right down to the ground. Only then do the snowflakes that have formed up in the sky also appear as such at ground level. Fog, or mist, on the other hand, is characteristic of the autumn. Tiny little droplets are formed when the warm, moist air close to the ground cools in the evening, creating clouds of mist or fog.

Where is the Earth's fresh water to be found?

The water on Earth comprises about 97% salt water and only about 3% fresh water. Fresh water is to be found in the ice of the glaciers in the polar regions and high mountain ranges, as well as in the surface water, meaning streams, rivers and lakes, and in ground water. It also includes the water vapour in the air.

What is a watershed?

A range of hills or mountains usually form a watershed where the streams and rivers flow down one side or the other. The large "European Watershed" runs through southern Germany. On the one side the water flows into the North Sea via the Rhine and on the other side it reaches the Danube and ultimately the Black Sea.

Try it: an evaporation experiment

When the Sun warms the air and the ground the water particles from the earth are released and swirl around in the air. This process is known as evaporation. The resultant water vapour is not visible to the human eye. You can observe evaporation by placing a glass upside down on a patch of grass. A great deal of water vapour is produced in the glass because the ground and the plants release water particles. The air becomes saturated with water vapour and the water condenses in the form of drops on the surface of the glass.

Climate and climate zones

What is actually the difference between weather and climate? Weather refers to the weather situation over a short period of time for a specific area. Scientists studying the climate monitor the weather situation over many years over a much larger area. The weather can change every day, but not the climate. There are zones all around the Earth where the climate is the same. These areas are known as climate zones. Within the climate zones, however, there are specific landscapes with characteristic flora and fauna.

An ice desert in a polar region

What do the polar regions look like?

The polar regions extend from the north or south pole as far as the respective polar circles. The winters here are extremely cold and although much warmer, the summers are still icy. It is always cold at the poles. It is very dry because the cold air is not able to absorb very much water vapour. Shrubs, lichen, moss, herbs and grasses grow in the adjoining tundra. The best known animals are the polar bears at the north pole and the penguins at the south pole.

● Polar region
● Boreal zone
● Temperate zone

Why is it cold at the poles?

When a specific amount of solar energy reaches a small area of the Earth at the Equator it creates warmth. Towards the poles, however, the same amount of solar energy reaches a larger area and it is therefore cooler there.

What is the boreal climate zone?

In the northern hemisphere the boreal zone adjoins the polar regions. The ground freezes during the long, cold winters and even in summer it is only the upper surface that thaws. There are huge pine forests and moors where brown bears and elks are to be found. Farming is not possible and the few people who live here survive by hunting.

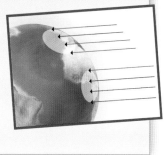

Pine forests, moors and lakes are characteristic of the boreal zone.

Stone desert makes up more of the Sahara than the sand desert.

Are there also subtropics in Europe?

The winters in the subtropics are mild and often also wet, while the summers are hot and dry. Deserts develop where there is very little rainfall. There are also stone or rock deserts in addition to sand deserts. Animals such as elephants and scorpions, and the plants too, are very well adapted to the extreme living conditions. Savannah is characteristic of the regions with little rainfall. This zone is also found in Europe in the Mediterranean region.

The Earth's climate zones

- Subtropics
- Tropics

Are there seasons in the tropics?

There are no seasons directly at the Equator. It is warm during the day and rains often. It is dry at night and somewhat cooler. Most of the Earth's plant and animal species are to be found in the rainforests. This is where the toucan lives and tropical palms and bananas flourish. Always humid, the tropics then give way to the savannah at their edges.

Mixed forests flourish in the temperate zone.

Can it also get cold in the temperate climate zone?

This climate zone is a band extending across both the northern and the southern hemispheres. Central Europe, for example, is in the temperate zone. The winters are cool but can also be rather cold, while the summers are mild to hot. Rain is possible at any time of the year. The seasons are especially distinct. The pine, deciduous and mixed forests are inhabited by squirrels, foxes, red deer and wild pigs.

Tropical rainforest

Polar regions, tundra, forest and steppe

If you were to travel from pole to pole you would encounter very contradictory climatic conditions. You would have to cope with icy temperatures in the polar regions, with hot days and cold nights in the subtropics, and with the evergreen, humid and hot rainforest extending right around the Equator. The animals and plants have adapted to the fundamental differences between their respective habitats. Only human beings inhabit almost all habitats from temperate to extreme.

Is there life in the polar regions?

The areas around the poles are too cold for plants. The few animals such as polar bears, arctic foxes and penguins obtain their food from the ocean as the polar seas are full of life. There are fish, seals and whales, with numerous bird species to be found on the coastline. Human beings live only in the northern polar region, the Arctic. The Inuit have adapted their way of life to the extreme conditions there. In the Antarctic, at the south pole, however, there are only research stations for scientists but not settlements.

Walruses live in the Arctic Ocean.

Do flowers bloom in the tundra?

The soil in the tundra is thin and mostly frozen. Trees are not able to grow here. Plants such as herbs and flowers have to develop their leaves and flowers during the short spring and summer and form seeds by the autumn. Most of the plants blossom at the same time and then the tundra is covered with numerous lovely flowers. Herbivores such as reindeer, musk oxen, polar rabbits and lemmings have adapted to the harsh conditions.

① Polar region
② The town of Ilulissat in the Arctic west of Greenland
③ Tundra
④ Tropical rainforest
⑤ Steppe in Africa

Guanacos live in the steppe regions of South America.

Autumn in the forests of Canada means a great many colourful leaves. Canada in fact has three climate zones: the forests belong to the boreal zone but there are also areas with a temperate climate and cold polar areas.

Are all forests the same?

We have extensive pine forests, mixed and deciduous forests and tropical rainforests on Earth, but also tropical woodland and woodlands with scrubland. Each forest has its own characteristic flora and fauna. In deciduous forests in spring, for instance, before the leaves

Steppe or savannah – what is the difference?

Steppe and savannah are grassy landscapes. Savannah is found in the tropical zone with wet and dry seasons. Grasses, shrubs and trees alternate within the landscape. In the dry steppe, however,

Fata Morgana

When warm air lies above cooler air then light is reflected at the interface of the two layers and you can see the sky reflected on the ground, for example. It can look like water, which is especially extraordinary in the middle of a dry desert. This kind of mirage is called a fata morgana.

have developed, the ground is covered with a carpet of early blooming flowers. In the rainforest, on the other hand, where there are no seasons and the trees therefore do not lose their leaves, it is always rather dark at ground level due to the leaf canopy. There is little undergrowth here. There are many reasons why we need forests. They store the greenhouse gas carbon dioxide, for example, and are important for maintaining our climate. Human beings are constantly felling ever more trees, however, in order to meet demand for wood and paper and to create space for housing and agriculture. This has many consequences. The destruction of forests also means the destruction of the habitat of the plants and animals that live in them.

it is hot in the summer and rather cold in the winter. It is generally too dry for trees. The prairies of North America, the Central Asian steppe and the pampas in South America are the most well-known. Grassy landscapes provide food for numerous animals: insects, birds, rodents as well as large herbivores – and of course there are also predators there who feed on these.

Not even shrubs grow in this steppe.

Savannah in Africa

29

Deserts, coastlines, oceans and lakes

Water is life. You become aware of just what that means when you see the tricks that animals and plants use to survive in extremely dry areas. Some animals obtain the water they require via their food alone while the dew in the early morning is enough for others. Many plants survive droughts as tubers or seeds in the ground. Trees such as date palms, on the other hand, grow long roots deep down to the ground water. This is not a problem shared by marine animals. Instead, they tend to have to cope with withstanding differing degrees of high water pressure.

Lighthouses emit light signals for ships close to the coast.

Are deserts always comprised of sand?

Deserts are areas that are so dry that only a few, if any, plants are able to grow there. We tend to think of sand deserts when we talk about deserts but not all

Which is stronger, the ocean or the land?

Ocean and land meet at the coast. Waves, as well as the rising and falling of the sea

sand deserts are entirely sandy. Only one fifth of the area of the Sahara is comprised of sand. The rest is rock, stone and gravel. Salt deserts are another kind of desert. Here, pools and marshy areas are covered with a solid salt crust. Animals such as camels, but also shrubs and grasses, have developed ways of withstanding the extreme dryness, heat and cold of the desert.

level, namely high and low tide, shape the coast. The ocean carries rock away. The rock is ground down into sand and deposited somewhere else as a sandbank, a headland or a sandy beach. This is how bays or lagoons are formed, for example. The ocean shapes caves, cliffs, arches and columns of rock. Nothing is able to counter the strength of the ocean.

Seahorse

The ocean waves gnaw away at the "Twelve Apostles" on the Australian coast every day.

① Salt desert ② Sand desert ③ Coral reef in the Red Sea ④ Lake Michigan is one of the largest lakes in North America and has a huge surface area of 58,016 km².

Is life evenly distributed throughout the ocean?

The ocean is a huge habitat. In comparison to the mainland, the living conditions are more consistent and also more uniform. Temperature fluctuations due to the seasons are much less marked. But how are living creatures distributed throughout the oceans? There is a considerable diversity of species along the edges of the continents, in coastal waters, because the herbivores find plenty to feed on here. This in turn attracts many predators. Large swarms

What water do lakes and ponds contain?

Lakes and ponds generally contain fresh water. They can be divided into different zones. Next to the bank zone is the shallow water. A variety of different plants grow in this bank area and it serves as a spawning and breeding area for many fish, birds, amphibians and insects. The adjoining area is the open water zone that is suffused with light. Lakes and wetlands form the habitat for countless

Frogs and birds live in the pond reeds.

④

⑤

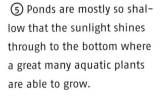

⑤ Ponds are mostly so shallow that the sunlight shines through to the bottom where a great many aquatic plants are able to grow.

of fish, for example, gather in open waters where nutrient-rich water from the depths is carried to the surface by currents. The deep sea, too, is a sought-after habitat. Crabs, snails, corals, worms, jelly fish and unusual looking fish inhabit the cold darkness.

animal and plant species. Geologically, lakes have a short lifespan because, over the course of time, they fill up with more and more deposits washed in by streams and rivers and worn away from the banks.

Volcanoes – the Earth breathing fire

A generally cone-shaped mountain of cooled lava and ash with a crater at the top – that is what many volcanoes look like. Some volcanoes are extinct while others slumber away peacefully for centuries before suddenly becoming active again. Some of them have been emitting lava, ash and smoke for hundreds of years. It is here that the force of nature, otherwise evident perhaps only with earthquakes, becomes clear. Even though volcanologists are constantly gathering new data, human beings are powerless when faced with the force of a volcanic eruption.

How are volcanoes formed?

Volcanoes have their origins in the Earth's interior. Tremendous pressure prevails in the Earth's mantle where temperatures reach up to 3000 °C. Some of the Earth's hard bedrock melts under these conditions and becomes liquid. This molten rock is known as magma. It is lighter than the mass surrounding it and so it forces its way upwards, collecting in hollow chambers in the Earth's crust known as magma chambers. The magma is able to reach the surface via cracks and fissures and is then known as lava. When the pressure in the magma chamber becomes too great the Earth's crust blows open, creating a volcano.

Mount Vesuvius, seen from Naples

Are there volcanoes that are especially dangerous?

Volcanoes like Mount Vesuvius in Italy often explode with tremendous force after being dormant for centuries. Chunks of rock and pieces of lava are thrown up into the air and large quantities of ash released. If the ash is flung high up into the atmosphere it is even able to influence the climate. Molten embers and clouds of ash can slide down slopes at tremendous speeds like an avalanche, destroying everything in their path. No less dangerous than Mount Vesuvius are volcanoes like Krakatoa: if the magma is very unyielding and the pressure in the magma chamber very high, the entire volcano could explode.

Vent

Lateral vent

Magma chamber

Cross-section of a volcano with the magma chamber, vent, lateral vent and an impressive ash cloud.

The Arenal Volcano in Costa Rica is one of the most active volcanoes on Earth.

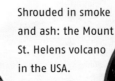

Shrouded in smoke and ash: the Mount St. Helens volcano in the USA.

Volcanic eruptions are especially spectacular at night.

The research carried out by volcanologists is not without its dangers.

Can volcanic eruptions be predicted?

Definite predictions of a volcanic eruption are not possible. There are, however, signs that can indicate an eruption. With some volcanoes, a number of minor tremors, imperceptible to us, can be measured prior to an eruption. The side of the volcano's cone can even be lifted up several metres when the pressure in the magma chamber increases. This was the case prior to the St. Helens eruption, for instance.

Mount Fuji

Mount Fuji, considered a holy mountain in Japan's Shinto religion, is regarded as one of the loveliest mountains in the world due to its uniform volcanic cone. It is a popular tourist destination in Japan.

What are geysers?

If we were able to climb down inside a geyser we would see a pipe extending downwards with ground water flowing into it. At its base the pipe is linked to a magma chamber where the water is heated. The huge column of water above it means that there is high pressure in the chamber and the water does not yet boil at 100 °C. The pressure decreases when the hot water rises up the pipe and this hot water, at a temperature of over 100 °C, vaporises immediately. A plume of steam and cooler water then shoots up out of the ground.

There are geysers in the Yellowstone National Park (USA), in Iceland and in New Zealand.

What are hot springs?

Ground water can be hot. It is heated by volcanic activity or by hot rock at great depths. This causes many minerals to be dissolved in the water. Sulphur compounds result in hydrogen sulphide being produced, which smells like rotten eggs. This water reaches the surface of the Earth as a hot spring. Often with curative properties, this water is frequently used as drinking water and for spa treatments. Even the Romans made use of its healing properties.

Winter in the Japanese Alps: the Macaque monkeys have a trick for making this habitat more pleasant – they warm themselves in the hot springs.

Extreme forces of nature

Volcanic eruptions, earthquakes, tsunamis or storms – these are natural phenomena with immense strength, which release tremendous energy. These are natural occurrences. They only become natural disasters when they endanger humans and animals, when populated areas are destroyed and when they endanger the livelihood of human beings. Man is powerless against these forces of nature. Scientists are working on ways of predicting such disasters. This at least gives the people living in the affected area the chance to reach safety.

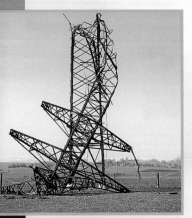

A hurricane is strong enough to tear down power lines.

ricane. A hurricane usually leaves a trail of destruction behind it. Trees are uprooted, power lines torn down, roofs blown off – and unfortunately there are frequently fatalities as well.

The suction of a tornado pulls everything upwards and carries it along for kilometres.

Storm or hurricane?

Scientists make a clear distinction between storms and hurricanes. A storm has wind speeds of between 74 and 117 km/h (kilometres per hour) and reaches Force 9 on the Beaufort Scale. Anything above that is a hur-

What is the "eye" of the hurricane?

Hurricanes are formed over tropical seas. Water vapour rises with the warm air, followed by air flowing in a lateral direction. Due to the earth's rotation, a huge vortex forms. In the midst of the vortex is the so-called eye of the hurricane, a point where it is calm. If you were to stand at this point you would in fact be able to see clear skies above.

The eye of the hurricane

The Beaufort Scale

The scale is named after its inventor, the English navy officer Sir Francis Beaufort (1774–1857). He developed the scale in order to determine wind strength without a measuring device and just by using indications on land or at sea. He introduced 12 wind strengths from calm (0) to hurricane (12).

Wind strength in Beaufort	Description	Wind speed (in km/h)
0	Calm	Below 1
1	Light air	1 – 5
2	Light breeze	6 – 11
3	Gentle breeze	12 – 19
4	Moderate breeze	20 – 28
5	Fresh breeze	29 – 38
6	Strong breeze	39 – 49
7	High wind	50 – 61
8	Fresh gale	62 – 74
9	Strong gale	75 – 88
10	Storm	89 – 102
11	Violent storm	103 – 117
12	Hurricane-force	over 117

Unpredictable in terms of direction, rotation speeds of up to 300 km/h, a diameter of up to several hundred kilometres, torrential rainfall, storm tides – a hurricane is able to flatten almost everything.

are slowed down once they run onto a flat coastline, however, and then they tower up as huge waves with tremendous power.

Why are earthquakes so dangerous?

Earthquakes are not as destructive for nature itself as you might imagine. They are a tremendous threat to human beings with their built-up environment, however. Panic ensues when the supposedly solid ground you are standing on suddenly starts to tremble, sway or even open up. The more built-up the human environ-

The coast of Japan was hit by a tsunami following an earthquake in 2011, causing unimaginable destruction.

ment is, the more fragile it becomes. Buildings collapse, gas pipes burst and fires result. Earthquakes in the ocean are often followed by tsunamis that flood what are often heavily built-up coastal areas. Human beings here can only try and save lives by means of ever newer technology such as earthquake-resistant building methods, for example.

What is a tornado?

Tornados occur over the mainland. They often develop from a storm cloud. The warm air below rises rapidly and the air begins to rotate more and more quickly. All of a sudden a kind of trunk extends out of the cloud and sinks down to Earth. A tornado is much smaller than a hurricane but it has enormous power. With wind speeds of up to 500 km/h in the interior of the tornado, it rips up everything in its path: trees, trucks, houses. It leaves behind a narrow trail of destruction.

Tornados occurring over the ocean or over large lakes are known as waterspouts.

What causes a tsunami?

Tsunamis are often caused by earthquakes. When an earthquake causes the ocean floor to rise, the mass of water above is also raised. As a result, the water spreads out in all directions as a wave front. The tsunami waves are barely noticeable in deep waters. They

Tsunamis move through deep water at speeds of up to 800 km/h. The speed decreases only once the water becomes shallower and that is when the towering waves are formed. A tsunami is always made up of a series of waves.

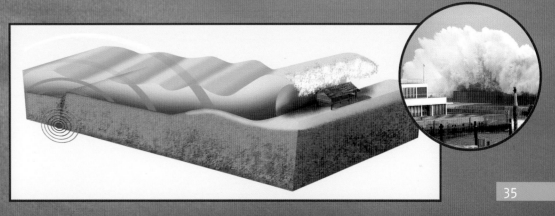

The origin of life on Earth

School children playing outside, a fish hiding in a reef, lions dozing in the sun, a carnivorous plant digesting a fly and wheat swaying in the wind – there is life almost everywhere. The Earth is inhabited by countless animal and plant species.

About four and a half billion years ago, however, none of this was yet in existence. There was no sign of life on Earth. Life in the simplest sense means metabolism and procreation.

How did life begin?

Scientists have found out a great deal but we are still not really able to say exactly how life began. It seems certain that the first forms of life began in water and that water was also an important prerequisite for this. It is possible that "black smokers", hot springs in the ocean depths, also played a special role. For several billion years the different forms of life were initially only very, very small. We would only have been able to see the unicellular organisms, which did not yet have a cell nucleus, through a microscope.

"Black smokers" on the ocean floor.

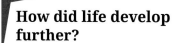

Plant photosynthesis is one of the foundations of life: together with sunlight, the green leaf colour chlorophyll converts CO_2 and water into sugar as well as releasing oxygen.

Carbon dioxide (CO_2)

Sugar (glucose)

Water

Oxygen (O_2)

How did life develop further?

Procreation is the driving force behind all developments in nature. Particular aspects can change slightly from generation to generation but what is important is whether they make a better contribution to survival than other characteristics. The animal, plant and fungus kingdoms as we know them developed over the course of time. There are also other life forms that are not so easy to categorise.

Stromatolites were formed by tiny, early life forms.

The time line shows the development of life through the geological eras. Mankind only appears at a very late stage and, in geological terms, man is therefore still young.

Archean	Proterozoic	Palaeozoic				
4600 million years – 2500 million years	2500 million years – 542 million years	542 million years – 251 million years				
For about the last 3800 million years: first unicellular organisms (bacteria) in the waters of the primordial ocean		Cambrian	Ordovician	Silurian	Devonian	Carboniferous

The marine turtle's ancestors once lived on land.

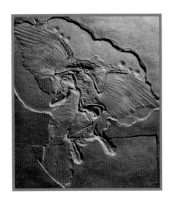

The primordial bird archaeopteryx still had reptile features.

The first two periods, the Archean and the Proterozoic eras, were both much, much longer than the other three, namely the Palaeozoic, Mesozoic and Cenozoic eras. In fact, a comparison of the five eras looks as follows:

How did life move from water to land?

Just visiting a swimming pool tells us that there are major differences between land and water. There were plants and insects on the land long before large animals appeared. Several years ago scientists discovered the fossil of a fish, the Tiktaalik, which was also similar to a four-legged animal. It thus constitutes a kind of interim form that makes it easier for us to imagine how the change between habitats was possible.

Where does our knowledge of prehistoric life forms come from?

No human being can report on prehistoric life forms of course. There are also not many traces that have remained preserved to this day. Palaeontology is the science concerned with prehistoric living creatures. It generally deals with fossils, meaning "excavated" in Latin. The main focus is on the fossilised traces and remains of early plants and animals such as dinosaurs. It is particularly in rock formed in the oceans that such fossils are found.

Quarry open to visitors

Here children have a great opportunity to look for fossils themselves using a hammer. They should always be accompanied by an adult for safety reasons.

What does evolution mean?

The natural scientist Charles Darwin

Each generation of living creatures passes characteristics on to the next generation, although these characteristics can change. This is how new species are gradually formed. In around 1860, the British natural scientist Charles Darwin described how those best adapted to their surroundings were the ones who survived. It is questionable, however, as to whether man is on the right path with his increasing interference with nature.

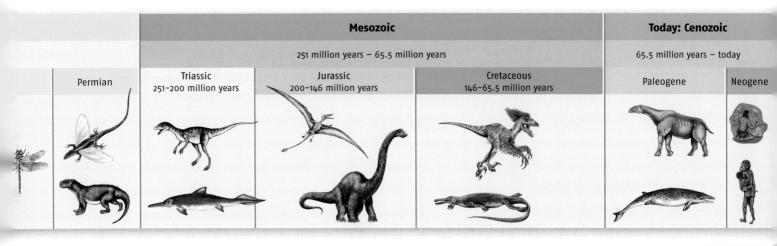

Permian	Triassic 251–200 million years	Mesozoic 251 million years – 65.5 million years		Today: Cenozoic 65.5 million years – today	
		Jurassic 200–146 million years	Cretaceous 146–65.5 million years	Paleogene	Neogene

The Earth as man's habitat

Human beings, gorillas, chimpanzees and orang-utans have common ancestors. Mankind today developed from these ancestors a few million years ago. Human beings like to see themselves as the "crown of creation" and they are indeed the only living creatures capable of such arro-gance. Life has always continued to develop over the course of time, however. Perhaps the descendants of present day human beings will one day stand in a museum and stare at us in astonishment.

① Australopithecus
(about 3–2.5 million years ago)
② Homo habilis (about 2.5–1.5 million years ago)
③ Homo erectus
(about 1.8 million years ago)
④ Homo neanderthalensis
(about 160,000 million years ago)
⑤ Homo sapiens
(for the last 200,000 years)

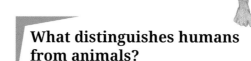

How did homo sapiens develop?

Human beings are thought to originate from East Africa. Man's initial stature was not yet comparable with that of modern humans. Man slowly developed his present day appearance over the course of two to three million years. "Homo sapiens", or "thinking man", has been in existence for about 200,000 years. Whether Neanderthals or "Homo erectus", it is important to note that the different development phases did not simply follow on from one another but sometimes occurred simultaneously.

What distinguishes humans from animals?

From a strictly natural science perspective, human beings are also animals. Nevertheless, we would certainly not say that our parents are two nice animals. The distinction between human beings and animals is not a simple one. Orangutan, for example, means "forest man". The genetic make-up of humans and of apes matches in many respects. Particularly when it comes to the right way of treating domestic and wild animals, we realise that human behaviour cannot simply be imposed upon ani-

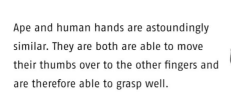

Ape and human hands are astoundingly similar. They are both are able to move their thumbs over to the other fingers and are therefore able to grasp well.

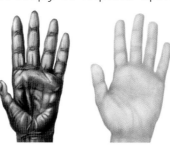

Chimpanzees are among man's close relatives.

Different cultures but with a great deal in common.

Cultural achievements require a common language. Even the building of the pyramids would not have been possible without it.

mals. Man's superior development is due to the development of his brain and of his intellectual faculties. He is able to pass a tremendous amount of information on to his descendants. It is impressive to see monkeys able to communicate by means of sign language, but they are not able to learn our complex language.

How does man influence the Earth?

It is only in the last few thousand years that human beings have begun to make themselves clearly visible on Earth. There were only 5 to 10 million people on Earth 10,000 years ago, as many as now live in the city of New York, for instance. They were directly dependent on nature and

No other animal is able to utilise and unfortunately damage nature like man.

were lucky to avoid being struck by lightning. However, improved nutrition meant that the number of humans subsequently increased significantly during the course of history. Forests were cleared, farmland and meadows were created. Today mankind is well on the way not only to influencing nature but to destroying it.

Where do language and culture come from?

Affection or anger is easily expressed without language. However, the information that the wounded bear is certainly still close by and that you therefore need to be on your guard is very difficult to communicate without words. And how would you explain "anticipation"? Language requires intelligence. Highly complicated physical changes were required in order for us to be able to speak as we do today, however. The tongue needed greater freedom of movement, for example. Someone who is able to talk can also pass on what they have learnt and knowledge can be built up. Language thus develops further and culture develops as the framework for a common way of life.

Communication by means of language even helped early human beings with hunting.

Climate change and protection

In as far as scientists are able to tell, the climate on Earth has changed repeatedly over the course of millions of years. The Earth resembled a giant snowball around 700 million years ago. The oceans were covered with ice and there was glacial ice even at the Equator. About 650 million years later, however, it was so warm that even the ice at the poles melted. Dinosaur tracks have even been discovered in the Antarctic. However, scientists are not always able to find an explanation for these at times extreme climate changes.

What is the natural greenhouse effect?

We all know that it is really warm in a greenhouse and there are several reasons for this. The sunlight and the solar energy penetrate the glass and are "swallowed" in part by the ground that is warmed in the process. Another part, however, is reflected from the ground as heat radiation, meaning that it is thrown back. This light is no longer able to pass through the glass as easily. It remains "caught" in the greenhouse, with the result that it becomes really warm. The process between the Earth and the atmosphere is similar. Some of the sunlight is swallowed by the Earth's surface, some is reflected as heat radia-

CO$_2$ is always produced by burning coal, gas or oil.

tion and the atmosphere then functions like the glass: it holds back the heat radiation, which gives us ideal living conditions of 15° Celsius on Earth.

The slash-and-burn clearing of rainforests also releases CO$_2$. Healthy forests absorb CO$_2$ through photosynthesis.

Climate & climate warming

There is in fact no such thing as a kind of global climate. There is a specific climate for a specific area but not for the Earth as a whole. Climate warming, however, means that the Earth's average temperature has become warmer over recent decades, by around 1°C at present.

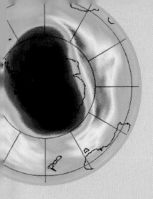

Storms and flooding can increase with climate change.

The **ozone layer** in the stratosphere prevents dangerous ultra violet radiation from reaching the Earth. This layer is being destroyed by rising gases from spray cans and refrigerants. This has led to the formation of an **ozone hole** over the south pole in the past.

How does man influence the climate?

The greenhouse gases are mainly carbon dioxide (CO_2), water vapour and methane. The warming increases if the proportion of these gases in the atmosphere rises. This is precisely what has happened over the last few decades. Human beings require more and more energy and burn coal, oil and gas for this purpose, emitting a great deal of CO_2. Food requirements are rising as the number of people living on Earth is constantly increasing. This means that there is a constant need to produce more. A great deal of methane is also produced through growing rice and through livestock farming. This makes human beings directly responsible for the increase in greenhouse gases.

What is the impact of temperature increase?

Nobody is able to make a definite assessment of the impact. However, changes are being observed even now and careful forecasts are possible: glaciers are melting more quickly. The area of ice at the poles is also decreasing. Storms and flooding, and also droughts, will increase in certain areas. Sea levels continue to rise.

Polar bears hunt seals and walruses from the pack ice. Polar bears do not find much to eat on land, however.

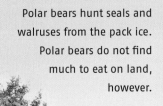

Are we able to protect the climate?

We can all help to reduce the rise in temperature by saving energy. Here are a few tips that apply to everyone: airing sensibly, meaning for shorter periods and therefore more often. Do not turn the heating up too high. Switch off lights when you leave the room. Ride a bicycle instead of driving a car. Use public transport like buses or trains. Buy regional foodstuffs as these have only travelled short distances.

Some regions are receiving less rain as a consequence of climate change.

Travelling by train instead of by plane protects the environment.

Natural resources and renewable energy

Human beings have been exploiting natural resources for thousands of years. We have found flint quarries where stone was quarried 5000 years ago. Flint was used for arrowheads, knives and scrapers. Salt, too, has long been a sought-after natural resource. The raw materials for a great many things in everyday use today come out of the ground. Different plastics are produced from oil; iron comes from iron ore and is then made into steel. Gold is used not only for jewellery but also forms part of many electronic components.

Cut diamond

Huge bucket wheel excavators in open-cast mines struggle through the landscape to mine lignite.

What makes natural resources so valuable?

Natural resources only become relevant as "resources" when they are required by human beings and particularly when they are required by a lot of human beings. A number of peoples were already using oil for lamps several thousand years ago. It was only in the 19th century, however, when conventional animal fats became scarce, that oil was used to produce lighting fuel. Benzene was produced as a by-product and with the invention of the combustion engine it came to be seen as the appropriate fuel. Oil became generally sought-after from this point on. Also, some natural resources such as gold or diamonds are very rare, making them even more valuable.

What are the natural resources we have?

Coal, copper and iron ore, uranium, gold and salt are well known natural resources. Less well known are tin and aluminium, for example. Tin forms a thin coating on tinplate cans. Everyone is familiar with aluminium as aluminium foil. We are often not aware that many rocks are in fact sought-after natural resources. Gypsum and lime, for example, are required for mortar. Granite is made into steps, floor slabs or work surfaces for kitchens. Limestone is used as gravel on roads.

Oil field

Gold rushes

In centuries gone by large gold finds repeatedly triggered what was known as a "gold rush". In America, for example, many people moved to places where there was said to be gold in the hope of becoming rich.

Many people then remained in the area even after the gold reserves had been exhausted. These were the origins of such well known cities as San Francisco or Denver.

The giant Three Gorges Dam in China is expected to produce as much electricity as 14 average nuclear reactors together.

A wind turbine converts wind energy into electricity.

ways. Electricity is generated using solar panels. Solar collectors, on the other hand, heat up water. In very sunny areas water can be heated to such an extent that electricity can be generated with the steam. Wind or hydro energy is also suitable for this purpose. Regenerative raw materials such as rapeseed or maize can be used for combustion to produce heat, which is then used to generate electricity. This produces only as much CO_2 as the plants have absorbed while growing. Geothermal energy is used for heating in particular but this technology is still in its early stages.

Why are renewable energy sources important?

Fossil fuels, meaning prehistoric fuels such as coal, oil and gas will certainly become exhausted at some point. However, limiting climate warming is another reason why we should try and use these fuels sparingly. Given that, in order to live, we need energy for a wide variety of processes, we need to be thinking about where this energy is to come from. Renewable energy is one step towards greater climate protection.

What renewable energy sources are there?

Renewable energy means energy sources that do not become exhausted. The Sun's energy, solar energy, can be used in two

Filling up on pure solar energy: solar panels and three solar collectors for heating water mounted next to one another on the roof of a house.

Does renewable energy also have disadvantages?

There are disadvantages even in the use of renewable energy. Valuable farmland is used for regenerative raw materials. The manufacture of solar panels alone costs a great deal of energy and wind turbines are not immune to criticism from nature conservationists. Dams do not always produce the energy promised and also have many ecological disadvantages. We still have a long way to go before the new forms of obtaining energy have been developed to such an extent that the habitat Earth remains protected.

Rapeseed is a regenerative raw material.

Farmland and water

There are about one million soil organisms living in a cubic metre (1 m³) of soil. These include bacteria and fungi but also animal soil dwellers such as snails, woodlice, mites and worms. They are all responsible for breaking down animal and plant remains and converting them into a humus layer extremely rich in nutrients. They also ensure that the soil remains crumbly, loosening and mixing it through. This enables farmland to store water and to retain air within it. Plants are only able to flourish on good soil from which they are able to acquire water and nutrients.

Why is fertile farmland valuable?

Nothing can be planted and nothing harvested without fertile farmland. Both livestock and human beings themselves would simply starve. The fact that the number of people living on Earth is constantly increasing means that greater yields also have to be achieved and the soil farmed ever more intensively, meaning more gainfully. More fertiliser is required and plants are bred to produce greater yields. Farmers prepare huge fields that they work with giant machines.

The larger the fields, the heavier the machines.

Is farmland under threat?

Intensive agriculture damages the soil. It becomes heavily compacted by the heavy machines and leaches more quickly. Huge fields without hedges and edging provide habitat for only a few animals and plants, thus decreasing biodiversity. Wind and rain are more easily able to carry off the soil from large fields and erosion results. The nutrients and the pesticides are washed out and pollute the ground water. The quality of the soil declines.

Many of the cornfields in the USA's Mid West are gigantic.

Plant fertilisers

The German chemist Justus von Liebig developed a water-soluble phosphate fertiliser in about 1847 and thus created the basis for the modern day use of fertilisers in agriculture.

Fields are often watered artificially.

Here every metre of ground is used to grow as much as possible. The terracing prevents the soil being washed away.

Why is fresh water so important?

Water is vital for life, for all living creatures and therefore also for us human beings. Wherever possible, people have always settled where they had access to water in the form of a stream or a river, for example. Wells were usually the focal point of the village. Water is used not only for drinking, cooking, showering, washing or for flushing the toilet. On a worldwide scale, agriculture uses the most water. Industry is the second-largest water consumer. Water is used as a solvent or a cleaning agent, for example, as well as for cooling. One thing is clear and that is that the manufacture of any one product requires the use of water, in whatever quantity.

Can water be distributed fairly?

There are some countries, such as Great Britain for example, where a lack of water is not prevalent. Unfortunately it would not help to bring water from other countries to countries such as Spain where there is a lack of water in some areas because it makes no sense to transport water across such distances. A shortage of water is often caused in part by human beings. Removing the causes can at least make a contribution to water being distributed more fairly. Contributing to climate protection also helps because scientists believe that the increase in droughts is caused by climate change.

The right to clean water

More than one billion people suffer from a scarcity of cleaning drinking water. The right to clean drinking water has therefore been declared a human right.

A canal strewn with refuse. The pollution of drinking water is another reason for clean drinking water becoming scarcer.

Is fresh water equally distributed across the Earth?

Water is very unevenly distributed across the Earth. Water is readily available in the north through to and including the temperate zone and at the Equator. In parts of the USA, Mexico and South America, but more especially in Africa, Asia and also in Australia, however, there are areas where a serious lack of water prevails. This is due primarily to the climate: the precipitation is too low and evaporation is high. The ground water found at tremendous depths in dry areas is often more than 1000 years old and is seldom replenished.

A dream for many children – having fun in an outdoor swimming pool.

Nature's records

Extremes of nature mean records. The widest, the highest, the coldest – all of these make us especially curious. The news that it can sometimes be cool even in the summer in London would be unlikely to surprise anyone. It is the contrasts possible on Earth that are especially fascinating. At just over 70°C the Dasht-e-Lut desert in south eastern Iran is considered the hottest place on Earth. The coldest place is said to be the Russian Vostok Station in the Antarctic. Temperatures of below –89°C have been measured here. That makes a difference of more than 150°C between the two.

Which is the deepest gorge?

When it comes to the deepest gorge we might in fact expect two opposing mountain sides with a steep descent between them. Many people are sure to think of the Grand Canyon in the USA, with a depth of up to 1800 m. The deepest gorge, however, is formed by the Kali Gandaki valley in Nepal. Its special feature is that it passes between two mountains that are more than 8000 m in height. From the valley floor the ascent is then about 6000 m. There are, however, gorges in the Alps that are distinctly more adventurous in appearance.

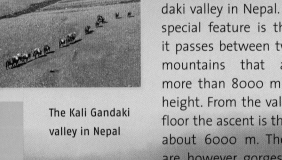

The Kali Gandaki valley in Nepal

How big is the biggest monolith?

A monolith is, as the name suggests, a large single stone. Ayers Rock (Uluru) and Mount Augustus in Australia are usually named as record-holders. Ayers Rock, 3 km long and 2 km wide, is better known but it is not certain whether it really is a monolith.

What extreme caves are there?

Caves can be characterised by very different extremes. The Sarawak Chamber forms part of the Good Luck Cave in Malaysia but is in fact anything but a "chamber". It is about 700 m long, 400 m wide and at least 70 m high. It is considered the largest known underground space to date. Such dark expanses are unfortunately difficult to photograph properly.

At 4810 m, Mont Blanc is the highest mountain in the Alps but is only about half as high as Mount Everest in the Himalayas.
At 8848 m, Everest is the highest mountain on Earth.

One of the longest passable caves is the Deer Cave in Malaysia.

Which is the longest river?

The length of the Nile in Africa is often given as 6671 km. The Amazon in South America is thought to be 6448 km long. However, scientists are still not able to agree on which is in fact the longest river.

The Nile as a shining, seemingly endless ribbon extending as far as the horizon.

How high is the highest waterfall?

The Salto Angel in Venezuela has a steep descent. At 979 m it is the highest "free falling" waterfall worldwide. The largest single step of the Salto Angel is 805 m high. The Salto Angel is named after the American who made them famous, Jimmie Angel. The local Pemon Indians call the waterfall Kerepakupai Merú.

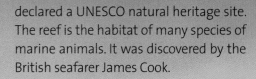

The fascinating underwater world of the Great Barrier Reef in Australia.

The Salto Angel is impressive in terms of its height as well as the mass of water.

Still more records

The Earth's inhabitants also produce records: the fastest land animal is the cheetah at more than 110 km/h. The largest living tree on Earth is a giant sequoia with a height of around 112 m. The Pyramids of Giza are among the oldest of Man's constructions. They are the only one of the Seven Wonders of the Ancient World still in existence.

A reef as a record-holder?

The Great Barrier Reef off the coast of Australia is the largest coral reef in the world. It extends over a length of more than 2300 km in total. It has even been declared a UNESCO natural heritage site. The reef is the habitat of many species of marine animals. It was discovered by the British seafarer James Cook.

Which desert is the driest?

The driest desert is found in Chile. It is not even particularly hot there but the Atacama Desert is surrounded by "rain barriers". The Andes mountain chain shields it from rain clouds. Deserts can even occur at the coast as cold ocean currents prevent rain clouds from forming.

The Atacama Desert, a place of extreme dryness.

Uluru or Ayers Rock is sacred to the Aborigines, Australia's indigenous inhabitants.

Index of key words

A

Alps 15, 16, 17, 33, 46
Andes 15, 16, 47
Astronomy 11
Atmosphere 12, 13, 22, 23, 24, 40, 41
Ayers Rock 46, 47

B

Beaufort Scale 34
Biosphere 5
Blue Planet 7, 12
Boreal Zone 26, 29
Brahe, Tycho 11

C

Caves 18, 19, 30, 46
Centrifugal force 9
Climate 6, 7, 13, 26, 27, 29, 32, 40, 41, 45
Climate protection 40, 41, 45
Climate zones 26, 27, 29
Columbus, Christopher 11
Continental drift 15
Continents 14, 15, 17, 31
Cook, James 10, 47
Copernicus, Nicolaus 11

D

Danube 19
Darwin, Charles 37
Desert 27, 29, 30, 31, 46, 47
Diamond 16, 42
Dinosaurs 7, 37, 40
Dunes 18

E

Earth's core 5, 9, 14
Earth's crust 5, 14, 15, 32
Earth's magnetic field 9
Earth's mantle 5, 14, 15, 32
Earthquake 14, 15, 16, 32, 34
Einstein, Albert 11
Equator 5, 8, 21, 26, 27
Eriksson, Leif 11
Erosion 18, 44
Evaporation 7, 24, 25, 45

Evolution 37

F

Farmland 18, 44, 45
Fata Morgana 29
Forest 6, 24, 26, 27, 28, 29, 39, 40
Fossils 37
Fresh water 24, 25, 45

G

Galilei, Galileo 11, 12
Gargarin, Yuri 7
Geyser 33
Glaciers 18, 25, 40, 41
Gold 42
Gondwana 15
GPS (Global Positioning System) 21
Grand Canyon 18
Gravity 13
Great Barrier Reef 47
Greenhouse effect 40

H

High tide 8, 9, 18, 30
Himalayas 16, 46
Homo sapiens 38
Hot spring 33
Humboldt, Alexander von 10
Hurricane 34, 35
Hydro energy 43

I

International Space Station (ISS) 6, 7

K

Kepler, Johannes 11

L

Lake 19, 31
Latitude 20, 21
Laurasia 15
Lava 14, 32
Legend 21
Liebig, Justus von 44

Life 4, 5, 8, 13, 19, 36, 37, 38
Limestone 17, 19, 42
Longitude 20, 21
Low tide 8, 9, 30

M

Magma 17, 32, 33
Map 6, 20, 21
Meteor 7
Meteorite 7, 23
Milky Way 12
Minerals 16, 17, 33
Monolith 46, 47
Moon 8, 9, 12, 13, 20
Mountains 15, 16, 17, 18, 24
Mt Fuji 33

N

Navigation device 20, 21
Neanderthal 38
North pole 8, 9, 21, 26

O

Oil 42, 43
Ozone hole 41
Ozone layer 23, 41

P

Pangaea 15
Penguin 26, 27
Photosynthesis 22, 36, 40
Planets 12, 13, 14
Polar bear 26, 41
Polar region 25, 26, 28
Pond 31
Precious stones 16
Precipitation 7, 24, 25, 45
Prime meridian 20, 21
Pyramids 39, 47

R

Rainforest 6, 27, 28
Renewable energy 42, 43
Rocks 5, 15, 16, 17, 18, 22, 33, 42

S

Sahara 27, 30
Salt water 25
San Andreas Fault 14, 15
Sandstone 17
Satellite 6, 21, 23
Savannah 27, 29
Scott, Robert Falcon 10
Seasons 8, 27
Solar energy 8, 26, 43
South pole 9, 10, 21, 26, 28, 41
Stalactite 19
Stalagmite 19
Steppe 28, 29
Storm 34, 41
Stratosphere 23
Street map 21
Subtropics 27, 28

T

Tectonic plates 14, 15, 16
Telescope 11, 12
Temperate zone 27
Tides 8, 9, 30
Tornado 34, 35
Tropics 27
Troposphere 23
Tsunami 35
Tundra 26, 28

V

Vikings 10, 11
Volcano 6, 14, 15, 16, 22, 23, 32, 33, 34

W

Water circulation 24
Watershed 25
Weathering 16, 17, 18
Wegener, Alfred 15
Wind circulation 22, 23
Wind energy 43